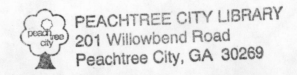

FOREWORD

"Frontiers of America" dramatizes some of the explorations and discoveries of real pioneers in simple, uncluttered text. America's spirit of adventure is seen in these early people who faced dangers and hardship blazing trails, pioneering new water routes, becoming Western heroes as well as legends, and building log forts and houses as they settled in the wilderness.

Although today's explorers and adventurers face different frontiers, the drive and spirit of these early pioneers in America's past still serve as an inspiration.

ABOUT THE AUTHOR

During her years as a teacher and reading consultant in elementary schools, Mrs. McCall developed a strong interest in the people whose pioneering spirit built our nation. When she turned to writing as a full-time occupation, this interest was the basis for much of her work. She is the author of many books and articles for children and adults, and co-author of elementary school social studies textbooks.

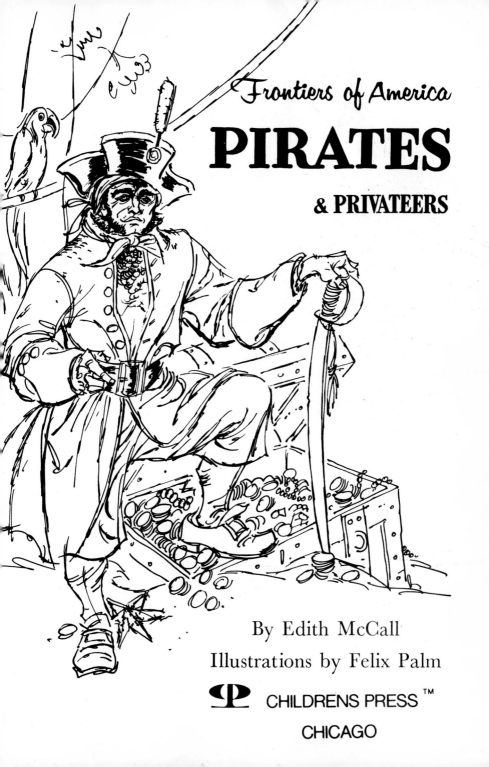

Frontiers of America

PIRATES

& PRIVATEERS

By Edith McCall

Illustrations by Felix Palm

CHILDRENS PRESS ™

CHICAGO

Library of Congress Cataloging in
Publication Data
McCall, Edith S
    Pirates & privateers.
    1. Pirates—Caribbean area—Juvenile
literature.   2. Pirates—U.S.—Juvenile
literature. [1. Pirates] I. Palm, Felix,
illus.   II. Title.
F2161.M13   910'.453   63-15637
ISBN 0-516-03360-3

New 1980 Edition
Copyright© 1963 by Regensteiner
Publishing Enterprises, Inc.
All rights reserved. Published
simultaneously in Canada.
Printed in the United States of America.

4 5 6 7 8 9 10 11 R 93 92 91 90 89 88

CONTENTS

PETER FRANCIS, BUCCANEER

There were pirates sailing the seas long before ships from Europe sailed to America. Columbus probably saw a pirate ship when he first became a sailor, going from one part of the Mediterranean Sea to another.

But the buccaneer, whose very name made people tremble with fear, was an American kind of pirate.

By the time the English colonies in America were sending shiploads of goods from their harbor cities, the buccaneers were the terror of every honest sea captain.

"Bloodthirsty," the sailors whispered, "that's what they are!"

The story begins in the West Indies, in the days when the Spanish, the English and the French were all trying to take the New World lands to be their own.

The Spanish had a strong hold on Mexico and most of the land south of it, and on most of the islands between North and South America.

About the time that the English colonies were beginning in Virginia and New England, a little colony of French settlers tried to live on an island in the West

Indies. A Spanish warship came and drove them away.

"Come, *mes amis!*" the bravest of the French settlers said, "we will sail to another island. There are plenty more."

So, loading all they could take with them in dug-out canoes, they paddled their way to the large island just southeast of Cuba, which now is shared by the countries of Haiti and the Dominican Republic. There were some Spanish settlements there, but there was plenty of room left over, especially in the northern part where wild cattle and wild pigs roamed.

"How will we live?" the French asked each other. "If we till the land, perhaps the Spanish will find our farms and chase us away before we can harvest our crops. We must find a quicker way to get food and something to trade for other things."

They found the answer in the wild cattle and hogs. They had learned, from the Carib Indians of the island where they had lived, a new way to fix meat so that it would keep without spoiling. The Indians smoked strips of it over slow-burning fires. The smoked meat was called *buccan.*

Soon the French were busy smoking meat, making buccan. They came to be known as the *boucaniers,* which in time became *buccaneers*. But as soon as they began a good trade in buccan, the Spanish again chased them away.

This time they moved to the island of Tortuga, just off the northern coast of Haiti.

They took along some cattle and hogs to smoke and soon were back in business. But six months later, along came the Spanish. They chased away the French, but when things were quiet again the French came back. This time they built a fort.

"Now, no man shall chase us away," their leader said. "Each man among you must swear that he will give his life before he will give up this island."

They formed a brotherhood of buccaneers. A newcomer to the camp had to swear on a skull, placed in the center of the black cloth in which it was kept wrapped between times, that he would stand by his brothers at all times. He pricked his arm with his knife and signed a pledge with his own blood.

"The Spanish are our enemies," they swore. "Any time we see them drawing near, we shall band together to fight them off."

COPY OF AN OLD MAP

The Spanish attacked the fort, but the buccaneers
were good marksmen from shooting the wild animals,

and they shot down all who came near their walls.

The next step was to go out to sea and attack the Spanish ships that came near. In those days, many of the battles between nations at war with each other were fought on the sea.

Since they had only their dugout canoes, the buccaneers had to plan how they would attack a big sailing ship. When they sighted a ship, they took their long muskets and sharp butcher knives and paddled out to sea under the cover of darkness. When dawn brought light and the crew began the day's work on board the big ship, each waiting buccaneer chose one man to be his own target.

Then, at a signal from their leader, they swarmed up the side of the Spanish ship, carrying their knives in their teeth and with muskets ready to shoot. Those who had pistols had them loaded and ready in their belts. The Spaniards, taken by surprise, were prisoners or dead in a few minutes' time.

Now the buccaneers had a sailing ship. Soon they took another, and another, finding the Spanish ships that were loaded with gold and jewels, taken from the Indians of Mexico and South America.

News of the buccaneers spread, and rough men

came from many places to join them. They had become not just protectors of their island, but pirates.

One day, soon after the buccaneers had begun roving the seas in pirate gangs, a big Spanish man-of-war, a smaller ship called a sloop, and a dozen little oyster fishing boats were moving slowly up the coast of Central America. The captain of the man-of-war stood on the highest deck of his ship and searched the blue waters of the Caribbean Sea for signs of other ships. Satisfied, he put down his long spyglass and turned to his ship's mate.

"Signal the fleet to drop anchor," he said. "We'll fill our water casks and get supplies ashore here in that little village."

"Aye, aye, sir," said the mate. He started to walk away and then turned back to his captain. He pointed off to the shore which they had passed not long ago as he said, "You noticed that small boat moving along the shore, didn't you, Captain?"

The captain turned away from the open sea and looked towards the shore. The fishing boats were pulling in close to shore. Out a little way from the fishing boats was the sloop which the man-of-war was guarding. The sloop was important, for on board it were all the pearls taken from the oysters the fishermen had netted that season. There were chests of pearls worth about one-hundred-thousand dollars on board the sloop, ready to be taken to Spain.

Moving up the shore, toward the fleet, was the dark shape of a small boat, its sails bound close to its single mast.

"That little shallop? Nothing to fear from that," the captain said. "It's just a trading boat, moving from village to village along the coast."

"Aye, aye, sir," said the mate again, and went about his work. The captain was right. Even if that little ship should be a buccaneer boat, the big man-of-war, with its cannons poking out of a long row of portholes in its sides and a big company of armed and trained fighting men on board, would have nothing to fear from it. What kind of pirates would use a poor little boat like that one?

The man-of-war dropped anchor much farther out from shore than the other ships did, for it could not float in the shallow waters. The treasure ship anchored a little nearer shore, and the fishing boats went up to the beach.

On board the treasure ship, one of the sailors leaned

on the deck rail, looking at the pleasant little village to which the ships' rowboats were already heading with empty water casks. The dark shape of the oncoming trading boat caught his eye. Some of its crew were rowing the boat out from the shore, skirting around the fishing boats and drawing nearer to the sloop.

"Lucky fellows," thought the sailor. "They'll soon be sitting in their own kitchens at home, eating fresh meat and newly baked bread, while we eat wormy ship's biscuit."

He watched the shallop, wondering why it was skirting so far around the fishing boats and coming so near to the treasure ship. Suddenly he stiffened. The men on board the little ship could be plainly seen now. They did not look like traders. They wore dark, dirty clothes that had not had the attention of a wife on shore for many a sea journey. The men's shirts were ragged, hanging over trousers that were cut off just below the knees. Their hair was long, mixing in with shaggy beards. But the really startling thing about the men was that each wore a bright cloth sash around his waist and another over his shoulder, called a *bandolier*. Sashes and bandoliers were packed with knives and pistols. No trader went about armed like that.

"Man the guns! The buccaneers are coming!" the sailor shouted.

The treasure ship had four cannons along each of its sides, and a crew of sixty men, many of whom were trained fighters. But it was too late for the cannons to hold off the men in the dark little boat. The boat was too close to be hit by them. A few men on the sloop quickly grabbed muskets and fired down at the pirates, but on they came, swarming up the side of the treasure ship.

Holding on with one hand, the buccaneers slashed with knives at any man who reached down to try to block their way. Only two or three pirates were forced back. About two dozen of them were scrambling onto the ship's deck, firing pistols and darting at sailors with drawn knives. The sailors fell back.

"Don't let them take us!" one brave young man cried out, and charged forward. Instantly, two pirates were slashing at him. The other men, staring at the awful sight of their friend dying before their eyes, pulled back farther.

"Hands high in surrender," ordered the buccaneer leader, and the sailors lined up.

"That's Peter the Great," one of the sailors whispered

to the man next to him. "He'll cut you in quarters and throw you into the sea, piece by piece, if you try to fight him."

Peter the Great, whose real name was Peter Francis, took over the treasure ship quickly. He kept a few of his men guarding the prisoners, after all guns and knives had been taken from them. The guards marched the sailors down into the hold in the lower part of the ship to lock them up.

"Weigh the anchor!" ordered Peter. "Stand by the halyards!" The men jumped into action. Sails filled with wind. Lines were made fast. The sloop got under way quickly.

The next step was to head for the man-of-war and try to take it by surprise.

On the man-of-war, someone noticed the opening sails on the treasure ship. He was sure the sailors on the sloop had decided to steal the treasure and were about to sail away with it.

"Mutiny on the sloop!" he cried out. "The crew is making off with the pearls!"

In a moment, orders were given on the man-of-war, and its sails, too, began to open.

Peter the Great saw that his hope of taking the big

ship by surprise was gone. Now the best thing he could do was to slip past the man-of-war before its cannons could be fired at him. The sloop was the faster of the two ships, and the pirates should be able to escape with the treasure.

"Head for the open sea!" he cried, as every inch of canvas caught the wind and the sloop moved faster.

Skirting around to keep out of reach of the cannons, the sloop drove ahead. The stretch of sea between the two ships widened every minute.

Peter the Great looked back at the man-of-war and his cruel face broke into a yellow-toothed grin. He had won his prize for sure. The clumsy man-of-war could never overtake the fast sloop. It was fairly skimming through the waves. Away back, the little shallop in which the pirates had attacked was washing in toward shore. Peter the Great wouldn't need it now. He had a fine ship, armed with cannons, from which to attack the next merchant ship he sighted.

First he would drop off the prisoners. Any island would do for that, or if none was sighted, the prisoners could be forced to walk a plank, hands tied behind them. With the end of the plank far out from the ship's side, no helpless sailor who had to walk off its end could stay afloat for long.

Then Peter the Great would take his treasure ship to a safe harbor he knew of, off the shore of Carolina, not far from a settlement in the English colony there. Peter Francis had a friend in that settlement who would help him get a good price for the load of pearls.

"A good day's work," he said, as he cleaned and reloaded the pistols he carried in his red bandolier. His knives already were wiped clean and tucked into his sash.

Peter raised his eyes to look back at the man-of-war, still trying to gain on the escaping treasure ship.

"Poor fools! Why don't they give up?" He laughed, and the black-bearded man who held the ship's big wooden steering wheel joined in the laugh.

Both of them had noticed the heavy black cloud that was moving in swiftly from the southeast. But neither of them dared to reef the sails. That would slow them down.

A moment later the wind hit them. There was a cracking sound.

"There goes the mast!" a sailor-pirate cried. Only the fast work of the men kept the mast, sails and all, from snapping off all the way and falling to the water. Sails were drawn in and ropes pulled tight to hold the cracked mast.

Almost as suddenly as it had come, the squall was over. And there was the man-of-war, moving in towards the crippled treasure ship.

Peter the Great knew that with the cracked mast, he could not hope to outride the big ship again.

"Stand by to fight!" he ordered. The four cannons on the sloop faced the oncoming battleship.

"Fire!" ordered Peter when the ship was close enough, and the cannons boomed.

The big ship shuddered as the cannonballs hit, but on it came, swinging around to aim its larger guns at the treasure ship. Its cannons boomed. Splinters flew from the side of the sloop. The treasure ship began to list to starboard as water rushed into a hole.

If the battle went on, pearls, pirates and all would go to the bottom of the sea. Peter the Great signaled that he would like to talk to the captain of the man-of-war.

In a few minutes, while some of the pirates manned the pumps to keep the treasure ship afloat and others worked to board up the hole, Peter and four of his fiercest-looking men rowed over to the large ship.

So mean and ugly did the pirates look as they climbed aboard the man-of-war, each man with a knife between his teeth, that the captain forgot he had the stronger ship and could be the master now. Fear of the buccaneers was much too great. He found himself agreeing to let the pirates go ashore in safety, if they would leave the treasure of pearls.

So the buccaneers went ashore unhurt, to get ready for another surprise attack on the next ship that sailed near them. Peter the Great finally captured a flagship of the Spanish fleet. On board was such a rich treasure that he gave up being a pirate, and settled down to live the life of a rich man on shore the rest of his days.

The gangsters of the seas grew stronger. Most of the leaders were French or English. They attacked Spanish ships more than others because England and France were at war with Spain, and because the Spanish were taking so many riches from Central America and Mexico and Peru.

Sometimes the buccaneers sailed northward to the North American coast where the United States would someday be. Word of how terrible they were spread to the people who lived in the English colonies there.

They heard of *Black Bart,* who, with twenty men, captured a big Spanish ship. He was kept from more robberies when a hurricane wrecked his prize ship. Then came *The Rock,* who was said to roast his Spanish prisoners on wooden spits, as others might roast hogs. Some buccaneer leaders attacked villages along the coast, as well as ships at sea.

Worst of all the buccaneer leaders was Henry Morgan, who led a regular army and navy of buccaneers. When the Spanish ships found the buccaneers were getting worse, they began to travel in great fleets, with large warships to guard the merchant ships. Morgan was not stopped.

Much of the Spanish gold and silver was put on board ships at a town in Panama called Porto Bello. Porto Bello was guarded by great forts and held by Spanish soldiers. Henry Morgan and his men attacked and took this city, coming by land. They killed everyone they met on the way. Their captured treasure was about a quarter-million dollars in Spanish "pieces of eight," and a fortune in silks, linens, velvets, jewelry and precious stones.

American colonists heard of all this. But they felt fairly safe, for the pirates worked mostly in the West

Indies and against the Spanish. They could not know then that the pirates were creeping northward, and soon would even be walking the streets of their colonial towns.

HENRY KING'S ESCAPE FROM A PRIVATEER

About one-hundred miles off the Virginia coast, the merchant ship *Providence,* flying the English flag, began to roll and toss on a sea grown suddenly stormy. The ship's mate, young Henry King, barked out orders.

"Shorten all sail to storm rig! Batten the hatches! Secure all lines!"

The ship was a busy place and a noisy one. The shouting of men rose over the wind's howl. Pulleys screeched as ropes were drawn through them, and tall masts, strained by the push of wind against the sails, creaked as they swayed.

When all was tightened against the storm, Mate Henry King reported to Captain Raddon.

"All battened down, sir, and ready to ride out the storm."

"Good," said Captain Raddon. "After our long wait to get started on this voyage, I would hate to lose the ship now."

The *Providence* had been loaded and ready to sail to Virginia in December of 1672. Now it was early April

of 1673. All winter long, the *Providence* had ridden at anchor in the harbor at Plymouth, England. In her hold were boxes and bales of warm clothing and supplies for the people who lived in the American colony of Virginia. There were sturdy leather shoes, and some fancy pumps with wooden heels, knitted stockings of all sizes, some cloaks, breeches, coats, collars and hats for men and boys, and a few bodices for the girls and women.

But mostly there were yards and yards of cloth, bundles of thread, and the pins, tapes, buttons and ribbons needed to make the cloth into everything from underwear to ballgowns. Most people made all of their clothes in those days.

Besides the dry goods, the *Providence* carried kegs of nails, a shipment of harness, some iron hinges and some cranes and pots for cooking in fireplaces, and a specially-made sidesaddle for a Virginia plantation lady.

If the lady wanted her saddle for the fall hunt, and her dancing pumps for the holiday parties, she must have been very disappointed, for the *Providence* was not allowed to leave the English harbor.

"I can't give you your sailing papers until there is a convoy ready to go," the harbor master told Captain

Raddon. "You can't go out onto the sea alone. If a Spanish privateer doesn't get you, a Dutch one will."

A *privateer* was a ship whose owner had been given papers from his country's government giving him the right to attack other ships, much as a pirate might do. It was part of war between countries in those days. England was at war that winter with Spain and with Holland. There were English privateers who attacked Spanish and Dutch ships, and Spanish and Dutch privateers who attacked English ships. Being a pirate was against the law, but being a privateer was lawful.

Finally, in the spring, there had been enough ships to start out together. Warships had taken them part way, past the waters of greatest danger. After that, the ships had sailed in small groups, but as they went farther and farther from Europe, most of them had separated and were sailing alone.

Captain Raddon had been careful to stay clear of the seas near the West Indies, keeping his ship on a more northern course.

"After safely passing the privateers, we don't want to risk meeting a buccaneer ship," he told Mr. Fox, the man who owned the dry goods and hardware. Mr.

Fox had come along on the journey to see that he got a good price for his goods in Viriginia.

Now, with the Viriginia harbors just ahead, a new danger had come. The storm grew worse as darkness came. The helmsman had himself tied to the wheel to help him hold the rudder steady. Winds tipped the poor little wooden ship until it seemed her decks would never straighten again. She rode the crest of a wave and then was tossed into the watery valley beyond. Rain drove hard through it all until the sailors' storm coats, hats and boots were running walls of water.

Suddenly it was over. The clouds broke and the moon peeped through. A gentle breeze took the place of the wild wind. The waves rolled on, but their fury was gone.

In his cabin, Captain Raddon was just beginning to rest after the long hard hours on deck when the cabin boy brought a message to him. It was about four o'clock in the morning.

"The watch reports a light two points off the port bow, sir," the boy said.

A minute later, Captain Raddon was on deck, studying the bobbing light through his spyglass. Henry King stood beside him.

"It could be a ship's lantern, Mr. King," the captain said. "It seems to be coming nearer." He passed the glass to King.

Henry watched the light a moment. As he watched, a tardy flash of lightning gave a sudden view of the shape of a ship. It seemed much closer than the bobbing lantern had appeared.

"Captain! It's a big ship, and it's armed," Henry said. He passed the glass back to Captain Raddon.

The Captain watched until another far off flash of lightning again showed the shape of the other ship.

"You're right, Mr. King. I thought we would ride out the night, but let's put some distance between us and that other ship and be out of sight by dawn. Set all sail. Change course to northwest by north."

"Aye, aye, sir," said Mate King. "All hands on deck!" In a few minutes, sleepy sailors were coming up from the bunks below to the wet decks. Sagging, water-soaked sails were soon unfolding.

Dawn's light brought bad news. The big ship was still in sight. Captain Raddon, studying it through the glass, was sure it was armed with cannons. It, too, had changed course, and was following the *Providence*.

"We've been sighted," he told Henry. "Are we doing full speed?"

"All she'll give, sir."

"I can't see the flag she carries yet. She is still about three leagues distant." That was about nine or ten miles.

An hour later, the big ship looked larger, even though the *Providence* was doing her best to outride it.

"She's after us all right, Captain," said King. "Do we stand any chance at all?"

The Captain put down his glass and shook his head. His shoulders sagged. After all the months he had waited to make this journey, his fine ship, cargo and all, would end up as a prize for some privateer. There would be no money to pay the men, for Mr. Fox would have no chance to sell his goods.

"Not a ghost of a chance, Mr. King," he said.

Henry gazed angrily at the growing shape of the armed ship. He felt sorry for Captain Raddon, and for Mr. Fox, too. It didn't seem right that an enemy country's ship should be allowed to take away all the goods on board and the ship, too, when the *Providence* was unarmed and hurting no one.

"There goes my chance for getting a ship on my own,

too," he thought. He had hoped that after another voyage or two, he could become a ship's captain for the company that owned the *Providence.* They were building more ships, and looking for good officers to put in command.

A few minutes later, the Captain could see that the privateer flew the flag of Holland. He made out its name, too.

"It's the *Slanswelvarn,*" he reported. "I believe that would be the *Commonwealth,* in English."

An hour later, the *Commonwealth* was alongside the *Providence.* Each of her guns was manned and ready to be fired. But Captain Raddon saw no use in having his ship hit by cannonballs when he could not defend it.

"Strike your flags!" the captain of the big Dutch ship called out. Raddon ordered the "Union Jack" taken down from its mast at the ship's stern and the ship's own flag lowered from the main mast.

A small boat was lowered from the *Commonwealth.* The captain and twelve of his men got into it, and soon they were on the deck of the *Providence.*

The Dutch captain held out a hand politely to Captain Raddon.

"My name is Delincourt," he said. He took a paper

from a waterproof envelope. "My letter of marque."

A *letter of marque* was the license a privateer carried, showing that the government of its country had given the captain permission to take enemy ships. One of the rules of the sea in those days was that this paper should always be shown. Otherwise, the ship might be considered a pirate ship, and its captain a lawbreaker. Captain Delincourt's papers were signed by the Prince of Orange, ruler of The Netherlands, which was at war with both England and France.

"Now then, sir, we shall have a change of crew," Captain Delincourt announced. He spoke in Dutch to the men he had brought with him, giving special directions to a slim, blond boy of about eighteen. The listening crew of the *Providence* decided that this boy, whose name was John Johnson, was to be their new steersman, and would be in charge of the ship. He was the only one who spoke English.

"We will see your cargo now, Captain," said Delincourt. Mr. Fox, looking very upset, went below with the two captains to show his cargo of dry goods and hardware. A few minutes later, Mr. Fox was forced to get into the Dutch small boat with the two captains and with ten sailors from the *Providence*. That left

Henry King and only six other men of the *Providence* crew aboard their own ship, along with the twelve Dutch sailors.

"I'm surprised they aren't locking us up," King said to John Champion, one of the crew left on the *Providence*. They watched the Dutch sailors take over the work of setting sail once more.

"What could seven men do against twelve big Dutchmen?" Champion asked. "Look at them — the only one that isn't oversize is the boy in charge. And he's well armed, you notice."

"So are all of them," said Henry. "I guess the Dutch captain isn't worried. This isn't much of a prize for him. What does a little merchant ship and a load of dry goods mean to him, after all? He doesn't even want the ship. He told me that tomorrow morning he will unload our cargo and give the *Providence* back to Captain Raddon."

John said, "I suppose we'll put in at Virginia to get something to take back to England. But poor Captain Raddon wasted a lot of time and money on this voyage."

Henry looked thoughtful. "John, there must be something we can do while the cargo is still on board."

"What can we do?" John shrugged.

At the wheel, young John Johnson felt ten feet tall. He had never been put in charge of a ship before. He would follow the *Commonwealth* as Captain Delincourt had ordered, and show him what a good officer he would make. But he wished the *Commonwealth* would reef its sails a bit. The *Providence* couldn't keep up with it. Already there was too much sea between the two ships.

Henry King walked up beside the boy. "What if you lose sight of your ship?" he asked.

"I have my orders," said Johnson. He kept his eyes on the Dutch ship as he spoke, and his mouth closed again in a firm line. Then he spoke again.

"I am well able to handle this small ship. We head back for Europe if we lose sight of the *Commonwealth*. I can chart the course without your help."

"Of course you can," said Henry. The boy said no more, and King turned away.

That night the spring sky was stormy again. The Dutch sailors had trouble keeping the *Providence* on course. Henry noticed a worried frown on young Johnson's brow when he turned the wheel over to another of his men and went below to rest.

When the light of morning came, Johnson was back

on deck. The *Commonwealth* was not in sight.

"Maybe when the mists rise, you'll see your ship again," Henry offered. "The captain was going to unload the cargo this morning. He shouldn't have left you so far behind."

"Captain Delincourt knows what he is doing," said Johnson, stiffly. But he looked long and hard through a small telescope before taking over the wheel.

That day ended and another. Still the *Commonwealth* had not been sighted. The cargo of the *Providence* was still safe in its hold. Johnson held his course for two days, trying to find the big Dutch ship. But on the morning of the third day, he ordered a turn to the east to begin the long journey back to Europe.

"We haven't enough food and water on board," King warned him. But Johnson was following his captain's orders.

They were well out in the Atlantic Ocean again when the man in the crow's nest called out, "Sail ho! Two points abaft the beam!"

Johnson borrowed Henry King's spyglass and watched as the ship came nearer.

"She flies the Union Jack," he said. "King, hoist your flag."

King ran up the English flag, as ordered, feeling mean as he did so. This was a common trick, trying to fool another ship's crew into thinking you were a friendly ship by flying the same flag. Some privateers carried flags of all the main nations, ready to put up any that matched that of the ship they were about to take.

Johnson called his eleven men together. He talked to them in Dutch. King listened, trying to decide what was being said.

"Johnson is going to try to be a hero," he said to John Champion. "You can tell by his face and the way he uses his hands that he is going to try to take another prize for his captain, maybe to make up for losing sight of the *Commonwealth*. He sure tries hard, doesn't he?"

"How will he do it without cannons?" Champion asked.

King said, "We shall see . . . . John, this may be just the break we need. Our boy leader is biting off more than he can chew."

The ship was coming willingly into the trap. It was a small merchant ship, and had even changed course to come nearer after the *Providence's* flag had gone up.

Both ships furled their sails as they drew close. Henry read the other ship's name — the *Barkely*. He saw the *Barkely's* captain speak to the mate on deck, and then go into the cabin. The mate held a speaking trumpet. Soon he called through it. "Where are you from?"

John Johnson had stepped up behind Henry, and Henry felt the push of the business end of a pistol in his ribs.

"Answer as I tell you," Johnson muttered. "And no tricks, or I'll shoot you down. Answer 'Of Falmouth.'"

This was easy for King to do, for it was the truth. The *Providence* did come from Falmouth, England. Then Johnson said, "Tell them we are outward bound from Virginia, and if they want to talk they should come over in a small boat." The boy's voice was thin with excitement.

King delivered the message. He could see that the *Barkely's* mate was trying to make sure that the *Providence* was really a friendly ship. He was squinting against the late afternoon sun, and having trouble seeing more than just dark shapes on the *Providence's* deck. He could not possibly see that Henry was answering at gunpoint. He seemed satisfied with King's answers.

"I am Bant, first mate of the *Barkely*," he called.

"Captain Prynne, master. He is below finishing letters he would like you to carry on to England. We need provisions to finish our journey, for we have been long at sea, put off course by the storms. Can you spare any water and flour?"

"Tell him yes, and to come and get them," Johnson said.

"Lower a small boat and come aboard!" King called.

The mate of the *Barkely* left the rail and disappeared into the cabin.

"They have provisions for us, Captain Prynne," he reported. The captain and the ship's merchant were at the table.

"My letter isn't quite finished, Bant," said the captain. "Will they wait?"

Bant said, "Beg pardon, sir, but if you could finish your letter on board the *Providence*, we could be getting the supplies and get back to the *Barkely* before darkness comes."

The captain picked up his paper, his quill pen and his bottle of ink. He and the merchant, the ship's doctor, three seamen and Bant got into the small boat that the sailors had lowered.

Henry watched them come near. If only he could

signal them that they were rowing right into a trap! But Johnson did not move from his side. The boy was trembling with the excitement of his daring, and Henry was afraid that nervous finger might pull the trigger on the pistol.

The visitors tied their small boat to the *Providence* and climbed the rope ladder that was dropped to them. As each man stepped on board, he found a Dutch sailor's hand clapped over his mouth and a gun poked into his back. The seven men were quickly searched for arms and then marched down to the hold.

Johnson looked a little worried. "I can't trust so many captives loose on the deck, but I've got to send a boarding crew over there to take the *Barkely* as a prize," he said, seeming to forget that Henry was not on his side. "I'll have to hold the ship overnight and unload it in the morning. It is getting dark."

He sent three of his twelve men, heavily armed, over to the little ship *Barkely*. From the deck of the *Providence*, the boarding seemed to go well, and it appeared that the three Dutch sailors would be able to hold the *Barkely* near by for the night.

King's mind was busy. He had a chance to get the *Providence* back, if only he could figure how to do it.

Now there were only eight Dutch sailors on board. There were prisoners down below who would be angry enough to help, if there were any hope of getting even with the Dutch crew. Through the night, he thought of what plan might work.

When morning came, Johnson called over to the *Barkely*, "We'll send you bread and water. When we have taken your cargo, you may have your ship back."

Because he had the keys to get into the hold where the cargo was kept, the *Barkely's* merchant was brought up to the deck and allowed to go with the seaman who rowed over to the small ship with a small barrel of flour and a cask of water.

King, watching from the *Providence,* saw the two men send the provisions up to the deck and then climb aboard themselves. He wondered where the three Dutch sailors were. As soon as the small boat had been unloaded, sailors scurried up the ratlines as if by signal. The sails opened and the *Barkely* began to move away.

"Stop!" yelled Johnson. Some sailors waved back at him, and the *Barkely* moved away as Johnson stared, his mouth open.

"My men must be circling it around to make the

unloading and loading easier," Johnson said, as he watched the *Barkely* swing around the bow of the *Providence*. "She'll be alongside in a few minutes."

But the *Barkely* swung away, heading for the Virginia coast as fast as the wind would push her. She was a trim little ship, and soon Johnson saw that there was nothing he could do to retake the prize that had slipped through his fingers.

He tried. He ordered King and the others of the captive crew to give chase to the *Barkely*. The Dutch sailors could not do it all alone. Somehow, the sails had never opened so slowly. Never before had so many lines been tangled. The *Barkely* was growing small in the distance before the *Providence* began to move. After three hours, Johnson, all the stiffness of pride gone from his slender body, turned the *Providence* eastward again.

King watched him closely. He almost felt sorry for the boy until he remembered that he, himself, should be in command of this ship in the captain's absence. He walked to the galley and saw that food was about to be sent down to the prisoners in the hold. The time had come to try his plan.

One man was on guard duty in the hold. King

slipped a note through to the prisoners while the man's back was turned, telling them to rush the guard when their food was brought down. Then he returned to the deck.

He had it all planned. His men were not armed, but there were only eight Dutchmen altogether now, and twelve Englishmen. That cargo might yet be saved and the *Providence* taken to an American port. If only it worked!

Nervously, Henry watched Johnson. The boy was his picked man. He seemed to have more spunk than all the other seven Dutchmen put together. Each free Englishman had been given one Dutch sailor to attack from the back. Help would come from the men in the hold, who would quickly look about to see where it was most needed. All they had to do was to get the guns and knives from the Dutchmen, and the *Providence* would be theirs once more.

All the men were ready. They heard the sudden sound of running feet coming up from the hold. Quickly, each man slipped up behind a Dutch sailor. Henry threw one arm around Johnson's neck, holding him in a choking hold. With the other arm, he pulled the boy's pistol from his belt and pressed it into his ribs.

"Drop your knife or I shoot," King said. Johnson did as told.

Quickly, King swung Johnson around, letting the wheel go untended. He had to see if the others were doing as well as he was. Their men were all bigger and stronger.

Some of the men were having a hard time. But the men from the *Barkely* rushed to help, and in less than a minute, the Dutchmen were lined up, unarmed. Not a shot was fired.

An hour later, a happy crew was sailing the *Providence* toward the American shore. The Dutchmen were in the hold.

Mate King said, "We'll set a course North by West. If we head for Virginia, we might meet the *Commonwealth* again. We'll head for a New England port, instead."

A few days later, the *Providence* found safe harbor in the Piscataqua River, which now forms the state line between New Hampshire and Maine. Portsmouth was just ahead.

There, in time, Captain Raddon and Mr. Fox found them. Captain Delincourt, thinking the *Providence* well on its way to Europe, had set them free, capturing a small fishing boat for them to use.

"I am a man of honor and not a pirate," he told Captain Raddon. "We shall see that you and your men have a way to get ashore."

The men from the *Providence* sailed off in the fishing boat, glad to be free but never expecting to see their ship again. Word reached Captain Raddon that his ship was in harbor, and his goods in a warehouse where Mate Henry King had moved them for safekeeping. Mr. Fox was more than pleased.

"I'll buy a stock of goods to send back on the *Providence*," he told Captain Raddon. "But on one condition. Henry King is to be mate, and report back to the company with me. By all that I believe in, I will make him master of the next ship the company sends to America."

CAPTAIN KIDD, PIRATE

Merchant ships found it harder and harder to get safely into and out of American harbors in the years after the *Providence's* long journey. Not only were there privateers lying in wait for them, sent by the nations that were at war with England, but the buccaneers had come northward into American harbors, too.

The "Jolly Roger," the black flag with the white skull and crossbones on it that had become the sign of the buccaneers, was seen often. People in the American colonies were growing upset about pirate ships that hid in American coves, and pirate captains who came into their cities selling stolen goods.

"Why doesn't the governor put a stop to it?" people asked. They soon learned that pirates had even been invited to the homes of one or two of the governors. Too many people were making money from the sale of the stolen goods for the pirates to be put into jail when they were seen. It was a bad situation.

"Something must be done. It isn't right!" was the feeling of most people.

That was the way Captain William Kidd felt, too. He had sailed along the American coast from his home in New York on many journeys as a privateer, and had taken prize ships from Spain and France when they were at war with England. He had had a brush or two with pirates, also, and was known as a man for robbers to keep away from.

But by the year 1695, Captain William Kidd was beginning to think about leading a more quiet life. He had a new wife and small children in New York City.

"No more privateering for me," he decided. "I'll take a few more trading journeys to England and back to make some more money. Then I'll settle down and enjoy my family and my home."

In the late summer of 1695, he set sail with a shipload of goods to sell in London. He did not know it, of course, but that journey was to lead him into trouble so great that in a few years' time he would be hearing a judge order him to be hanged as a pirate. People in his own America would be telling tales of "The Terrible Captain Kidd."

"They say he wrote ransom letters in the blood of women and children he kidnapped and murdered," people would be saying then. "He climbed onto ships of honest merchants with his cutlass between his teeth and murder in his heart. He buried hundreds of chests of gold and jewels, all stolen by him and his black-hearted men. Now their ghosts come to frighten away anyone who tries to dig up the treasures."

When Captain Kidd docked his ship in England in the month of October, 1695, he went to London to sell his cargo. On the street he met another American, also from New York. It was Mr. Robert Livingston, and he seemed glad to see Captain Kidd.

"Well, Captain Kidd! You're just the man I am looking for. Come over here and sit down. I'd like to talk to you about some important business," said Mr. Livingston.

Captain Kidd learned that Mr. Livingston and a group of other men, mostly men who owned merchant ships, had met with the King of England to talk about the trouble that pirates were giving their ships. The buccaneers were not only in the West Indies and along American shores, but were also attacking ships sailing around Africa on their way from Europe to India. In fact, the buccaneers had taken over the big island of Madagascar just east of Africa.

"The owners of the East India Company are losing

many ships to the buccaneers," Livingston said to Captain Kidd. "And you and I both know that things in the American colonies are not going well. You also know that the governor of New York is doing nothing to get rid of pirates. In fact, it is no secret that he has friends who sail under the *Jolly Roger.*"

Livingston stopped a moment. Kidd grunted and waited for him to go on. He knew that Livingston wanted something of him, and he was not at all sure that he was going to like it.

"Now, my friend, you yourself have fought many a battle with pirates when you were privateering. You're known as a man who can handle a ship well. Who better than you can go out and rid the seas of pirates once and for all?"

Captain Kidd started to speak, but Mr. Livingston stopped him.

"Now, wait a minute — there is one more bit of news. A new governor has been chosen for New York. He will be behind you all the way in this. So will the King, and the men of the East India Company, as well as your fellow Americans."

"I have no desire to risk my life any more," said Captain Kidd. "I am planning to settle down to a quiet life and enjoy the years that are left to me."

But Mr. Livingston would not take no for an answer. He got Captain Kidd to promise to go to meet Lord Bellomont, the new governor who would soon be sent to New York.

"You must agree to do it," Lord Bellomont said. "We will fit out a fine ship for you, and give you plenty of sailors and fighting men trained in the British Navy. You will have a letter of marque giving you the right to take French ships as prizes, too, and you and your men shall have a good share of the prizes."

Captain Kidd went right on saying no, politely but plainly. He sold his goods and bought more to load into his ship. But when he tried to sail out of the Thames River to head back to America, the King's officers would not give him sailing papers.

"Sorry, Captain Kidd," he was told. "We have orders to hold back your clearance papers. Orders of His Majesty."

Captain Kidd wasn't told the reason, but he guessed it. He saw that he had no choice but to go out on the pirate-hunting journey. But when he went to see the man-of-war that had been promised as a ship, he found a smaller ship being fitted out with guns.

"The Navy needs all the warships for fighting on the high seas," Kidd was told. "But this merchant ship, the *Adventure Galley*, will have fine fighting power."

Captain Kidd spent the winter in England, waiting for the *Adventure Galley* to be made ready. Early in April he was ready to set sail. On board were 155 picked men from the British navy, going along with the understanding that they would not be paid a salary, but would be paid in shares of the prizes they helped capture. That way, every man would do his best, for if there were no prizes taken, there would be no pay for anyone.

The *Adventure Galley* was ready to start down the river to the open sea. Early in the morning of sailing day, a small ship's boat, rowed by six men in the uniforms of British sailors, came up alongside the *Adventure Galley*.

"Hail, Captain Kidd!" called out the lieutenant in charge.

When Captain Kidd came to the rail, he was handed a paper.

"Orders to take one hundred men from your crew," the lieutenant said.

Captain Kidd's face grew red. He sputtered and

swore. But boatload after boatload of his best men were taken from his ship. He tried to find more men ashore, but the navy had already taken every able-bodied man to be found.

So Captain Kidd set sail for America. He would find more men in New York, he thought.

On the way, after a stormy voyage, a small ship flying the French flag was seen. It was easily captured, but the cargo was only salt and fishing tackle, being taken to the fishing banks off Newfoundland.

"It will buy supplies for our long journey," Captain Kidd said, "even though it is not much of a prize. There will be better ones later."

Finding good men in New York was impossible. Captain Kidd had to take beggars, and thieves who had been locked up in jail. He found some men who knew ships and sailing, but most of the men he signed up were "green" hands. Even the ship's doctor was not to be counted on, for he drank too much. But the crew was the best Captain Kidd could find. He set sail with 160 men, leaving New York on September 6, 1696.

"We'll swing on through the West Indies looking for pirate ships," he told his officers. But somehow, all the pirate ships kept out of sight. So did the French ships.

It was the same way as they crossed to the Madeira Islands, off the coast of Africa. No prizes were taken. At Madeira, while the *Adventure Galley* was being made ship-shape, a ship came limping into harbor after coming northward around Africa.

"The storms were terrible. I don't envy you your journey around the Cape of Good Hope," the captain told Captain Kidd.

The men had hoped that this ship would turn out to be one they could take as a prize. They began to grumble. So far they had nothing to divide among them at all. But Captain Kidd took only three barrels of sugar from the other ship, and for it he exchanged a bundle of canvas with which to mend sails.

They headed along the African coast, southward.

"Sails!" was the cry on December 12, and the men got their guns ready for an attack. But before long, they put them down.

"English ships," Captain Kidd said.

"We could take them, anyway," said a gunner named Moore. "Ain't none of us goin' to get rich this way."

Captain Kidd turned on his heel without bothering to answer. Three weeks later, on New Year's Day, they were nearing the Cape of Good Hope. Captain Kidd came upon a group of sailors gathered around Moore on the deck that morning. Moore's whiny voice was raised.

"I say we need a Captain what kin *find* prizes if we don't happen on none!" Moore was saying. There was a sudden silence as the men saw Captain Kidd, and the group broke up. Captain Kidd pretended he had not heard.

Rounding the Cape in bad weather was hard work for every man on board and there was no time for anything but managing the big square-rigged ship. Northward they went towards Madagascar, through quieter seas.

"Now we'll find pirate ships. We are heading into their nest," Captain Kidd said. But even at Madagascar, they had no luck at all. It was as if the French navy had all gone home, and every pirate ship sunk to the bottom of the sea.

As they were about to leave Madagascar, to head into the route the richly loaded ships from India took, they saw a French ship.

"We'll take it," Captain Kidd said. The captain of the French ship came on board the *Adventure Galley* after surrendering. He fell over as he stood before Captain Kidd, and in less than fifteen minutes he was dead.

"Cholera," the ship's doctor gasped.

"Cholera!" the men cried out, and backed away. "We've taken a fine prize! The crew's got cholera, and we'll all be dead if we stay near."

The *Adventure Galley* moved on around Madagascar towards the Indian Ocean's trade routes. Again Captain Kidd found Gunner Moore talking against him.

"No prizes, no pay," Moore was shrieking. "I say we have been on this ship long enough without prizes!"

"Right!" cried out a stronger voice. It was that of Tom Palmer, a sailor who had been with Kidd since the ship was fitted out near London. "For a year and a half, I've been on this ship with nothing but promises!"

The first mate, George Bullen, stood by, listening and doing nothing to stop the talk. Kidd slipped out of sight without being noticed. His heart was heavy. Surely his luck would change soon. Otherwise, he would never be able to hold his crew.

But the time had not yet come. About fifty of his men died of the cholera. And when ships were sighted, they were found to belong to the East India Company. On they went, day after day.

They stopped at a place called *Matta* to get water and wood. It was a wild place, and a native killed one of Kidd's sailors. As people often did in those days, the crew returned killing for killing. Some of the sailors set fire to a house. Two days later, Gunner Moore went ashore at another place to buy corn, but he was held captive, for the story of the killing and burning had traveled.

Natives came to Captain Kidd, asking for money for Moore's return.

"He is hardly worth buying back, but I'll pay the ransom," Captain Kidd said. Moore was returned. It would have been better for both Moore and Captain Kidd if the *Adventure Galley* had left him there.

September came again. The *Adventure Galley* had been at sea more than a year without taking a prize, except for the cholera ship. Then one day a lookout shouted, "Sails!"

The men's steps quickened and there was a cheerier note in their voices as they moved about the decks getting the guns ready for firing and taking positions to handle the sails when orders came. Up went a

French flag on the ship. Captain Kidd raised a French flag, too, to draw the ship nearer.

The other ship's captain was unsure of the *Adventure Galley*. He tried to move away.

"Fire!" ordered Captain Kidd. And then the ship's French flag came down and the Union Jack went up. Captain Kidd could read its English name, *Maiden*.

"No prize," he said. But Mate Bullen had already gone to board the *Maiden*, and was returning with her captain, her mate, and some pepper and coffee from her cargo.

Before they could be sent back, the *Maiden* set sail, not knowing her captain and mate were about to be sent back and the ship allowed to go on. The *Maiden* headed for a port, where her crew told the English officers that Captain Kidd had turned pirate. Word had also reached the officers there of the burning of the village house and the killing of the native, except that the story had grown to burning down a whole village and killing all the people.

"Captain Kidd has turned pirate," they reported in letters sent to England.

Two Portuguese attacked the ship of bad luck next, and some of the *Adventure Galley's* crew were killed before she could get away. The next ship sighted was English.

"Take her anyway!" screamed Moore. Almost all the men seemed willing to go along with Moore's ideas. The talk went on, but Captain Kidd would not allow them to attack the English ship.

"I can't hold them much longer," he muttered as he listened to them discussing the matter.

One evening, Kidd came on deck. Moore walked right toward him, while the other men gathered in a body behind him.

"It is two weeks since we've seen a ship, and you let that one go by," said Moore. He planted himself directly in front of Captain Kidd. "We demand that you give the ship to Mate Bullen."

Captain Kidd pushed at Moore and tried to walk by. "Out of my way, you dog! Is it my fault that no enemy ships have been sighted? Now step back and all of you go about your business."

Moore stood firmly. "No. Step aside, Captain Kidd, and let a real man take over the ship."

Captain Kidd's temper rose. He picked up a wooden bucket that was on the deck. "Get out of my way, you

lousy dog!" he shouted, and he swung the bucket at Moore.

Moore ducked and the bucket caught him on the head. He fell to the deck. Three days later, Moore was dead.

Captain Kidd knew that he had had to put Moore down to hold his ship, but he had not meant to kill him. If he had wanted to kill him, a better way would have been to draw his gun and shoot the man down. That would have settled the mutiny in a hurry.

The grumbling went on, but no one dared to face Captain Kidd. Each day, the captain wondered if he would be able to hold on through the day. Then at last, his luck changed. A French ship came along, and the *Adventure Galley* took it as a prize. Its cargo was not gold and silver, spices and cloth of gold from India. It was only sugar, cotton and two horses. But it was a start, and the captain had given up his French pass to Captain Kidd as proof that the ship was a French ship.

"We'll call it the *November,* after the month in which we took it," Captain Kidd said. "Now, men, let's follow it with another prize."

But it was February when the next prize was taken. The *Adventure Galley* was beginning to leak and wouldn't have held out much longer. Even Captain Kidd was about to give up when more sails were sighted, like a great white cloud riding low on the water.

The creaking *Adventure Galley,* as if bringing forth her last bit of strength, put on a burst of speed and moved toward the great ship. The crew sent a volley of cannonballs across the bow of the other ship, to stop her.

"She flies a French flag," said Captain Kidd. "Ready to board her, men!"

As fierce as any pirate crew, the men of the *Adventure Galley* swarmed onto the *Quedah Merchant.* The captain came back to the *Adventure Galley.*

"Now look, Captain Kidd," he said in English. "My name is Wright. This isn't really a French ship, and not a lawful prize for you. We used a French flag because that is what you ran up."

Captain Kidd felt his heart sinking as if it were a ball of lead. But he'd have proof the ship was English before he gave it up.

"Let me see your pass, Captain Wright," he said.

Captain Wright plainly did not want to show his papers, but he had no choice. He held out a pass signed by the French government officers.

"Surrender your ship, sir," ordered Captain Kidd, and his heart was light again.

The cargo was all the men could hope for. There were bags of gold and silver, chests of jewels, and a great pile of rolls of fine silk cloth of many colors. Besides these riches, there were barrels of sugar, bales of cotton and some iron and, of course, the ship itself.

It was a beauty, a fine big sailing ship in much better shape than Captain Kidd's ship.

"We'll name this one the *Adventure Prize,* men. We'll take it back to America right away."

But the men eyed the gold greedily. It was a long wait until they reached America again, and most of them had nothing there that they cared about. One night, many of them slipped away, including Mate Bullen and the ship's doctor. A pirate named Robert Colliford had his ship near by and sent word he could use good men. With the little handful of men left to him, Captain Kidd had no chance of capturing Colliford.

Colliford laughed when he was asked why he didn't attack the *Adventure Prize,* which Kidd was now using as his ship.

"I don't attack *fellow pirates,*" he said, meaningfully.

Kidd reddened when he heard this. So that was

what they were saying about him! He headed for the West Indies with the *Adventure Prize,* followed by the *November.* There he learned that he had been charged with becoming a pirate, for it was reported that his big prize ship really belonged to the ruler of India, and not to France. He was also charged with the murder of Gunner Moore and with killing natives and destroying their village.

"It is a good thing I have the two French passes to prove that I took these ships lawfully," Kidd said. He told friends in the West Indies, "I am going to leave the ships here while I go up to talk to Lord Bellomont and straighten out this trouble. I'll send for the *Adventure Prize* as soon as I can."

He bought a small ship, hid the big prize ship in an out of the way cove, and headed north to New England. He found a lawyer first of all, and told him the story.

"Here are the French passes that prove I acted in a lawful manner. Any captain would have taken steps to stop a mutiny as I did with Moore, and I don't believe I can be charged with murder. The story of the native village is not true."

The lawyer took the passes. "There's one thing you should know, Captain Kidd," he said. "England signed

a peace treaty with France just about the time you took your last ship."

"Word had not yet been spread of a treaty," said Kidd. "Now if you will go to see Lord Bellomont, maybe we can straighten this out."

The lawyer left, taking the passes with him. While he waited to hear what was to happen next, Captain

Kidd stopped his small ship alongside an island called Gardner's Island. He gave some of the goods he had brought north with him to Mr. and Mrs. Gardner, and buried a chest of gold somewhere on the island. All the things were later turned over to the governor.

The news that came back to Captain Kidd shocked him. Lord Bellomont, even though he had been given the passes, was charging him with piracy and murder. He pretended that there never were any French passes.

A few weeks later, Captain William Kidd heard the judge in a court in England where he was tried without being allowed to defend himself, say, "Guilty! He shall be hanged by the neck until he is dead."

For a long time, Captain William Kidd's body, pecked at by birds and tossed by winds, hung there for all to see.

"That is the terrible pirate, Captain Kidd," people

said. "He was the fiercest pirate ever to sail the seven seas. Murdered women and children he did . . . . . ."

Captain Kidd, privateer, was dead. Captain Kidd, King of the Pirates, lived on and on, in stories about him.

BLACKBEARD'S CAPTURE

Almost twenty years had gone by since the sad end of Captain Kidd's pirate-chasing journey, and there were more pirates than ever before.

In the city of Charles Town, South Carolina, the most important city in the southern colonies, a lady pulled her two children closer to her and hurried them towards the carriage where a dark-skinned driver waited.

"Don't point, John. Come along, Mary. Yes, I know, my dears. Those men are pirates. Come now, quickly."

Pirates had made of Charles Town a regular calling place on their way north from the Indies. They came into Pamlico Sound at Ocracoke Inlet and left their ships in any of a hundred little hidden harbors.

As the driver helped the lady and her children into the carriage, the lady said, "It is getting so that it is unsafe for a lady to leave her home, Joseph."

"Yes, ma'am," said Joseph. "And I hear them a-tellin' about how that man Blackbeard has his ships blocking the Charles Town harbor right now."

Young John, looking like a small-size copy of a man in his light blue satin knee breeches and dark blue coat, poked his sister.

"Mary, did you hear that? Blackbeard is coming here!"

Mary shuddered. "He's horrible. I'm afraid of him."

John said, "I'd sure like to see him. He's got this great big bushy beard, black as night, and long black hair, so his face hardly shows. Guess it's so ugly he wants to hide it. And he curls and braids his whiskers every day. He buys yards and yards of pretty satin ribbon to tie at the ends of the braids."

Mary couldn't help but giggle at the thought. But she felt safer now, for the pair of fine horses was taking them nearer home and farther from Charles Town each minute.

John went on. "But you should see how fierce Blackbeard looks when he's about to capture a ship. You know what he does, Mary? He sticks matches — you know, like we have in our Betty lamps — long strings that burn, except that he soaks them in something that gives them a greenish light — well, he sticks them in his ears and under his hat brim and then he lights the ends. In the dark, he looks like a horrible beast coming at you."

John turned and made a sudden clawing motion at his sister, twisting his mouth into an ugly shape as he did so.

"Oh, John — you scared me!" Mary cried.

Their mother turned to them. "That's enough about pirates now, John. Talk about something else."

"Just the same, I'm going to sea when I grow up, and fight pirates like Blackbeard. I'll capture them all, I will."

His mother sighed. She hoped there would be no pirates left when John was grown, but it was a sad thing now. She knew it to be a fact that pirates were invited to the homes of some of the merchants in Carolina, for business men made good money in handling the stolen goods. No one seemed able to stop them. Just lately, the King had given governors the

right to pardon pirates if they would give up being pirates. When the fighting with France had ended, England was at peace with other nations for a few years. Many of the privateers had become pirates in those years. Then some gave up piracy because they would be hanged if they were caught, as Captain Kidd had been. Under the King's pardon, many of them were leaving the sea now. But the worst of the pirates went right on with their robbing and killing.

Joseph had heard correctly. Blackbeard's four ships were in the Charles Town harbor on that May day in 1718. No ship was safe. Blackbeard had just captured two that tried to leave the harbor and three that were about to enter it. Now, no ship either entered or left Charles Town harbor, for the news had spread that the *Jolly Roger* held the port.

John was right, too, about how ugly Blackbeard was and how he made himself more frightening with lighted, slow-burning matches. Blackbeard's real name was Edward Teach. He had left England years before as a privateer, but had become the most horrible of pirates. He called himself *the Devil,* and even tried to prove to his men that he really was the Devil.

He dared them once to go down into the hold of his ship with him, where he had placed pots of brimstone and started them burning. The hold was filling with the terrible biting, choking smoke, and only three or four would go down with Blackbeard.

"We'll see who can last the longest breathing the air that is like that of the Devil's own kingdom," Blackbeard said as he bolted the hatch.

Soon the men were begging to be let out. When Blackbeard saw that they would have to be carried out if he did not open the hatch, he unbolted it and shoved each man up the ladder to the hands of the men who waited on deck to pull them out. Blackbeard alone was not choking and gasping for air.

"That proves it," he said. "Now you know who I am."

His men believed him, and none dared go against Blackbeard's will.

The pirate leader and his crew of about 400 men were settling down for a vacation around Charles Town while their ships were being put into good condition. So that they would be perfectly free to come and go, in plain sight of Governor Johnson who was known to hate them, Blackbeard worked out a plan.

He went to see Governor Eden of North Carolina,

knowing that Governor Eden had had some dealings
with pirates before. Blackbeard dressed himself in his
favorite clothes for the visit. He wore his bright red
silk coat with the wide velvet cuffs that turned back to
the elbows and had lace ruffles as a shirt front. The
full skirt of the coat partly covered yellow satin

breeches. He wore white silk stockings and low shoes with giant silver buckles on them.

He had spent extra time on his beard that day, twisting it into great curls and tying the ends with bright ribbons. It parted over his chest to show the bandolier fitted with pistols. He wore this in addition to a wide belt which held a longer pistol, his razor-sharp knife, and his long cutlass.

Of his face, all that showed made him look more ugly. His lips were thick and loose and his teeth yellow. His beard covered the rest of his face, except for his nose and red-rimmed, puffy eyes. On his head was the black felt hat that most pirates wore.

The people of the town of Bath saw Blackbeard in all his finery, followed by twenty-five rough, dirty pirates, march up to the front door of the governor's house. All of the pirates went inside. Governor Eden found Blackbeard, with the twenty-five pirates standing behind him, in his office when he was called there a few minutes later.

"Guv'nor," said Blackbeard, "I've come to take the Act."

"Aye," said the men behind him.

The governor sniffed as he smelled the dirty pirates.

Dressed in light blue satin clothes of the latest French style, and wearing a powdered wig, he looked almost ghostlike beside Blackbeard. He seemed a bit nervous as he sat down behind his large desk. His secretary, Mr. Toby Knight, seated at a smaller desk off to one side, found his own hands damp and wiped them on his lace handkerchief before taking up his quill pen. If Blackbeard had come to "take the Act" that meant he would have to write out the pirate's pardon, known as the "Act of Grace."

"Well, Blackbeard, I am pleased to see that you now understand the mistakes of your past and wish to be pardoned," said Governor Eden. He had just had a report that the man who stood before him had taken twenty-seven ships in the past month.

"Yes, your honor," said Blackbeard. "I'm going into the business of salvaging ships from now on."

Salvaging ships was honest work of raising wrecked ships from the ocean floor, or bringing in ships that had been tossed about by storms and could not sail alone. Governor Eden looked sharply at Blackbeard for a moment when he heard this news of Blackbeard's plans. In that moment, Blackbeard's puffy right eye closed in a wink. Governor Eden looked down again quickly.

"Raise your right hand, gentlemen," he said. The pirates then made their promise that they would no longer take part in piracy. All but Blackbeard filed out of the room.

Then Blackbeard sat down on a little French chair that creaked under his weight. He clapped his rough hands onto his knees, spread wide apart, and said, "Guv'nor, the law says that lost ships must be reported to you. Now I lives by the law, and I'll be reporting to you the ships that I salvage. Now, as I sees it, there is no use for any good ships to be lost drifting around in that great big ocean, out there, so long as Blackbeard and his men are near at hand to salvage them."

He stopped a moment and then he slapped his knee. "Haw, haw, haw!"

A heavy silence followed his rough laugh. Governor Eden cleared his throat. "You mean, of course, you will pull ships off the rocks," he said.

"Too late to salvage them, once they hits the rocks, yer honor. I tells you about them, and you tells me I have salvage rights." Again came the wink.

Blackbeard went on. "Now you are a hard workin'

man, as I sees it, Guv'nor. It seems to me that you should get a present now and then for your hard work."

He and Governor Eden had an understanding when he left. Perhaps the governor reasoned that the pirate would do as he pleased, anyway, and some of the money might as well come into Carolina. Blackbeard, the pardoned pirate, became Blackbeard the ship salvager, but it was hard to tell the difference.

He was seen on the streets of Carolina towns often, and even invited to parties. But no one asked him back to the same house again, for he thought it great sport to suddenly draw two pistols at a dull moment in a party, fire wildly with them either over the heads of the people or under a table and see the people jump and hear them scream. He laughed when everyone scrambled for cover. He crippled one of his own captains by shooting him in the knee when he was playing this "game."

At last, in May, Blackbeard was tired of his vacation. By that time, letters from Carolina people had gone to the King of England, asking for help in getting rid of the pirate gangs. They moved away from Charles Town harbor, and once again honest trading could take place.

Blackbeard and his captains moved along the coast,

"salvaging" ships. But the pirate leader was growing restless. He wanted to take a long ocean journey.

"We'll need some bandages and medicines to take with us," he told his captains. "We'll go back to Charles Town to get them."

The first luckless ship to head out, just as Blackbeard reached the entrance to Charles Town harbor, was starting on a journey to England. One of the passengers was a Mr. Wragg, a member of Governor Johnson's council. The pirates boarded the ship and Blackbeard singled out Mr. Wragg.

"I am going to hold you, Mr. Wragg, and the rest of the passengers, until the four hundred pounds' worth of medical supplies that we need are brought to us," said Blackbeard, holding poor Mr. Wragg by the ruffled shirt front. With his free hand, Blackbeard waved a paper on which were listed the wanted supplies.

"If these things don't come back to us right away, I'll kill you all," he said.

A merchant named Marks was the one chosen to do the errand. He was sent ashore in a boat rowed by pirates. He did not come back the next day, nor the one after. Blackbeard ordered all the passengers lined up on the deck.

"Mr. Wragg," Blackbeard said to the councilman, "if the supplies are not here tomorrow, you and all the others shall lose your heads."

He thrust his ugly face close to Mr. Wragg's, and then went down the line doing the same to each shrinking prisoner.

"Shake in your boots, landlubbers!" he roared. "You won't be alive to shake much longer."

A messenger, most welcome to the frightened passengers, came the next morning. "Mr. Marks' boat turned over and he was almost drowned," the messenger reported. "But he is gathering the supplies now. They will be here tomorrow."

That saved the passengers for another twenty-four hours. But on the following afternoon, an angry, impatient Blackbeard ordered the prisoners lined up once again.

They were all frightened when they saw him. He marched back and forth in front of them, wearing only bright colored pants and a vest and sash. His great black, hairy arms swelled with muscles. In his right hand he gripped his long, shiny cutlass, and he waved it at the prisoners as he walked by them. Then he jumped atop a keg of gunpowder and slashed back and forth with the sword as he cried out, "Who'll be the first? I'll cut off every one of your heads before the day is out!"

No one stepped forward to be first.

"Step up, now, or we'll drag you here!" roared Blackbeard.

One of the prisoners did step forward then, and the pirate's yellow teeth were bared. But the prisoner stayed back just out of reach of the terrible knife.

"Captain Blackbeard, sir," the man said. "We have all had a meeting. We decided that, since no one on shore seemed to care what happened to us, we will join your pirate gang. Why should we care about the people of Charles Town? They don't care about us, so we'll help you take the town!"

Everyone held his breath to see what would happen next. The brave prisoner stood there, trembling with fright at what he had done. It was a desperate chance he took, and a last hope for himself and his friends to stay alive through the day.

Blackbeard stood for a moment with the cutlass raised. Slowly he lowered it and stared at the prisoner. His thick lips squeezed together as he thought over the offer. Then he stepped down from the keg.

"Weigh the anchor!" he called. "Load the guns! The tide will turn in an hour. We'll take all of Charles Town — and then we'll decide what to do with you." With these last words, he swung about and pointed his knife at the prisoners once more.

The ships began to move across the sand bar at the edge of the harbor as the tide rose. The first of them had entered the harbor when a small boat was seen coming toward it. At last, almost too late, the supplies were being sent.

Suddenly Blackbeard was impatient to get away from Charles Town. He took the supplies on board his ships, helped himself to the chest full of gold coins that he found in the merchant ship, and to its food supplies. And then he and his men were gone. The passengers who had so barely escaped with their lives found themselves going back ashore at Charles Town, almost too weak to walk ashore

The anger of the people of Charles Town did not die down this time.

"He'll be back," they said, "and we'll be ready for him."

Governor Johnson wanted to get ships ready to meet Blackbeard upon his return, but South Carolina did not have enough money to fit them out. He knew that Governor Eden would not help him.

"We'll ask Virginia for help," he decided. He knew that Virginia's governor, Alexander Spotswood, was a strong and brave man, and that Virginia was the richest of the near-by colonies.

Governor Spotswood posted signs right away. *One hundred pounds reward for Blackbeard's head. Ten pounds for each of his men,* the posters read. These excited the young men, and when the governor fitted out two ships, at his own expense, he had no trouble getting brave young men to man them. He chose officers and fifty-five trained men from the Virginia armed forces.

Word came that Blackbeard had dropped his three other ships and many of his crew, and was on a ship called the *Adventure,* sailing alone, and heading for the Carolinas once more. Lieutenant Robert Maynard, in charge of Governor Spotswood's two fast little boats, the *Pearl* and the *Lyme,* was ready to meet him. He knew that a surprise attack was all that would work against Blackbeard. His two boats were of the kind that could go into shallow water. They did not carry heavy cannons, but his men were all well armed with guns, knives and cutlasses such as the pirates carried.

The two small ships lay in waiting, hiding in an inlet. There they would stay until Blackbeard's *Adventure* was also in off the high seas.

As the *Adventure* dropped anchor, a messenger was rowed out to it in a small boat, just as darkness came.

"Captain Blackbeard, here's word for you from his honor, Secretary Toby Knight," the messenger said.

Blackbeard read the note. "So — a fancy young lieutenant is coming to take me prisoner, and we should leave quickly. Haw, haw, haw!" Blackbeard bellowed out his laughter. He doubled over and slapped his knees. He was still laughing when the messenger returned to the rowboat and headed back towards shore.

When darkness came, Lieutenant Maynard had his two sloops moved to a place just outside the cove where the *Adventure* lay at anchor. There they waited for the first gray streaks of dawn. In the dim light, they could make out the mast of the *Adventure,* reaching above the treetops around the bend. Maynard ran up the Union Jack and signalled that anchors be lifted.

The *Pearl* led out, with sails open and men at the oars, too. Speed counted now. Even so, one of Blackbeard's watchers spotted the two little ships coming into the cove and called Blackbeard to the deck.

The big pirate had spent the night drinking, laughing often over the good joke of a "fancy young lieutenant" capturing him. His eyes were more red-rimmed than usual, but his brain was working quite well. He gave orders to bring the *Adventure* about so that her guns could hit the *Pearl*. Then he went to his cabin and made himself ready to kill a lieutenant. He put on his hat and tucked the ends of his slow-burning matches under the brim and around his ears. He tested his cutlass for sharpness and then lighted the ends of the matches.

Blackbeard's men made their first mistake before their captain returned to the deck. They ran the bow of the ship onto the edge of a muddy bank. There it hung.

Lieutenant Maynard knew he must act fast and get in close to the larger ship before the cannons could blast the *Pearl* apart.

"Throw everything overboard so that we won't go aground," he called, "and pull hard, men!" Overboard went the water kegs, the untied anchor and the sand bags which were used to give the ship weight. Maynard had the wheel and swung the rudder so that the *Pearl* stayed out of the range of the cannons, moving in towards the *Adventure's* stern.

"Stay low, out of musket fire," he told his men. As the *Pearl* slid in alongside, Blackbeard appeared on deck, his head a green-lighted devil's invention. He was very angry to find his ship had gone aground. He swore loudly and then picked up a jug of rum and took one great swallow. He lowered it, wiping his whiskery mouth with the back of his hand, and roared, "I'm coming to get you, you fancy young lieutenant! I'll lop off yer head!"

Maynard was thinking hard. Musket fire could pick off his men before they reached the *Adventure.*

"Below decks, all of you, with muskets ready," he ordered. "The second we touch the *Adventure,* rush up. The Jolly Roger won't be flying much longer!"

Maynard had to keep moving to avoid being hit himself as he guided the sloop under the stern of the *Adventure.*

The ships touched. Instantly, pirates leaped down onto the *Pearl's* deck. The men rushed up from below, fired their muskets and dropped them. Pistols and knives would be weapons for the rest of the battle.

The quick bang of gunshot, the clatter and clash of

knives and swords and screams of pain filled the air. Man to man, Virginia fighting men and pirates battled it out to the death.

Blackbeard had been first to leap onto the deck of the *Pearl*. Maynard was ready for him. Both drew pistols and fired at the same instant. The younger man made a quick sidestep as he fired, and the pirate's shot went wild. Maynard's pistol shot caught Blackbeard in the face, and for a moment, the pirate reeled backward. Blood was streaming over the great black beard. But he was coming toward Maynard again.

Pistols were not repeaters in those days. After one shot they were useless until there was time to reload. Each man tossed aside his gun and reached for his cutlass. Maynard's sword was lighter in weight than the pirate's and he could move more quickly. The big, black-bearded pirate slashed down heavily with his cutlass, and Maynard knew that if he hadn't moved quickly his skull would have split in two from that one blow.

All over the deck, the men battled, thrusting and yelling, for a few minutes that seemed an hour. Then the *Lyme* had moved in, while the pirates were busy trying to kill their attackers. With the careful aim of trained fighters, the men on the *Lyme* fired muskets and pistols. Several pirates fell. Quickly then, the rest of the fighting men joined in the close fighting. Now there were two Americans to each pirate, and before long, the pirates lay dead.

All but Blackbeard.

Maynard had said he wanted to take him alone. On they fought. Maynard could not have taken his eyes from that horrible, bleeding, bearded face and those red-rimmed burning eyes if he had wanted to. It was as if the devil himself were holding the young lieutenant.

Maynard was caught by a slash at the leg, and for a moment thought he would fall. The pirate, his fang-like teeth bared, making a yellow slit in the black and blood-red of the face, raised his cutlass high. He was bringing it down with all his might. Maynard got his balance again just in time to slash at the cutlass, and turn the blow aside so that it only nicked his shoulder. As Blackbeard swung from the blow, the young lieutenant sent home a slashing blow and another.

The pirate was badly wounded, but he did not fall.

"Die, you Devil!" Maynard shouted. Again and again he ducked Blackbeard's blows, swinging and thrusting at every chance. His breath was almost gone and he felt himself weakening. Still Blackbeard stood there. Once again he raised his heavy sword for a blow at Maynard's head, even though he was cut in at least twenty places.

With his last ounce of strength Maynard slashed out at the pirate's neck. He heard Blackbeard's sword clatter to the deck. But, with a bleeding hand, the pirate pulled a pistol from the bandolier under his beard and aimed at Maynard's chest. Maynard, gasping, could no longer move.

The pistol fired. Maynard, falling, heard the shot.

Then, at last, a glazed look came into Blackbeard's eyes. The pistol dropped to the deck. The ugly man, more terrible to see than ever before, lunged forward and fell. One last glow of greenish light went out as Blackbeard's life ended.

The men rushed forward. Maynard still breathed. The pirate's last shot had splintered the deck.

The next day, the battered *Pearl,* followed by the *Lyme* with the pirate ship in tow, sailed back toward Virginia to report to Governor Spotswood. Lieutenant Maynard, bandaged and as lame as his ship, rested on the stained deck as another officer took charge.

Many of the crew were as bandaged as the lieutenant,

but all were cheerful. On the bow of the *Pearl* was a
warning to pirates that the rule of the Jolly Roger was
coming to an end. It was the head of the cruelest pirate
of all, the mighty Blackbeard.

STEDE BONNET, LANDLUBBER PIRATE

At the same time that Blackbeard was bringing terror to the American coast, another pirate was getting his start. His name was Stede Bonnet and he had never been to sea. In fact, he was a gentleman and a soldier and knew nothing about ships. But he, too, was to soon send shudders down the spines of the people of Carolina.

One day he walked out of his fine home in the West Indies and slammed the door behind him.

"Talk, talk, talk!" he said. "Must she talk *all* the time? She scolds and fusses at me as if I were a naughty little boy instead of the husband who keeps her in fine silk dresses. One of these days - - -"

Stede Bonnet didn't tell anyone what he would do "one of these days." He just went ahead and did it. He bought a sloop and hired a crew of seventy men. People thought he was going into the shipping business, even after he had the name *Revenge* painted on the ship.

"When are you setting sail? What will your cargo be?" people asked him.

"You'll know one of these days," answered Stede. But he was gone before they knew. In the middle of the night, he set sail. The first news people had of the *Revenge* was that it had attacked a ship at sea, that it was flying the *Jolly Roger,* and that — of all things — Stede Bonnet had become a pirate!

The soldier-gentleman-turned-pirate had a hard time at first. He was seasick for weeks on end. He didn't understand the language of sailors, and his men knew it.

"He doesn't know a bowsprit from a jib," his men said, and laughed behind his back. They were a tough lot, and most of them had sailed the seas for many a year. They thought it strange that their captain had to trust the mate to give all the sailing orders, and some began to plan how they would get rid of the "landlubber."

But Stede Bonnet, as soon as he got over the sea-sickness, set about studying. He had books on ships and sailing, and he had accounts of pirates. He wanted to do everything right. He hated the idea of making prisoners walk a plank, but if that was the way pirates handled them, then Stede Bonnet would make prisoners walk the plank.

The men tried to mutiny, but only once. Bonnet

pulled out his pistol and blew the brains out of the first man to step out of line. He ordered the rest whipped, and they took their punishment. They had forgotten that their captain had learned to be a dead shot while he was in the army, and that he had learned to give orders there. They decided to forget about mutiny. Besides, Captain Bonnet always wore a pair of loaded pistols in his belt.

Soon after he had proved himself master of his ship, Bonnet came upon Blackbeard. It was just at the time that Blackbeard was settling down for his stay in Charles Town harbor. The *Revenge* dropped anchor near Blackbeard's ship. Soon, a messenger came inviting Stede Bonnet to call upon Blackbeard in the big pirate's cabin.

"Good," said Bonnet. "I will call on him. As fellow pirates, we will have much to talk about."

Stede dressed in his brightest shirt, sash and trousers. He put on his cuffed boots, his bandolier and his finest hat. But as he stepped inside Blackbeard's cabin, he felt strong hands grasping his arms. His pistols and knives were taken from him. Blackbeard leaned back in his chair and laughed, pointing a pistol carelessly in Bonnet's direction.

"Sign the *Revenge* over to me," he ordered.

"But I thought you —" was as far as Bonnet got. The evil gleam in Blackbeard's eye made up his mind for him. He signed over the *Revenge*.

"Now that is the right way to behave," said Blackbeard. "And as a reward, I'll let you keep the ship's log. Even a landlubber can learn to do that."

Bonnet was with Blackbeard's men all through the long stay in the Carolinas and until Blackbeard decided he wanted to sail with just one ship again. He gave the *Revenge* back to Stede.

"I've got a much better ship than that old sloop," he said. "Take it back, landlubber. And stay out of my way from here on."

Bonnet set out again to be a pirate, but this time he was a wiser man. And while he had been obeying Blackbeard's orders, he had worked out a secret plan that he hoped he could someday try.

He heard of many pirates who were "taking the Act," as Blackbeard had pretended to do. England was at war with Spain again, and the King thought that by pardoning pirates, he could get many of them to sail against Spanish ships as privateers. Part of Bonnet's plan was to ask for a pardon and papers of a privateer.

He hid his sloop in a cove and went to ask for a pardon. It was quickly granted. Now he needed a crew for the *Revenge,* as he had only a handful of men who had stayed with him. Luck was with him, for he found some of Blackbeard's men on an island where the pirate had left them when he no longer needed a big crew.

"How would you like to get even with Blackbeard?" Stede asked.

Their shouted answer made it clear that they were ready to go on the trail of the man who had left them to starve on the island. Away they sailed, learning where Blackbeard had been seen, and taking a number of prize ships as they went. Bonnet had learned much about pirates' methods from Blackbeard, and soon word spread that a pirate named Stede Bonnet, pretending to be a privateersman, was robbing and killing all who crossed his path.

The *Revenge* was closing in on Blackbeard when Lieutenant Maynard battled the ugly pirate to the death. Bonnet's men felt cheated of their chance to get even, but they sailed on with Bonnet.

The people of the American colonies, having rid themselves of the worst pirate of all, were ready to go out after any others who dared to come to their shores. Bonnet had a narrow escape or two, and knew that sooner or later he would be trapped.

"We'll change the ship's name," he decided. They hid in a cove long enough to paint the hull and to put on a new name, the *Royal James*.

"A good English privateer's name," Bonnet said. "Call me Captain Thomas from now on, men, and we'll get a fresh start."

They went out on a tour in which they took several ships, pretending to be privateersmen, but Bonnet didn't turn in any of his prizes to the government. He treated his prisoners so badly that soon word spread that the *Royal James* was a pirate ship and not a privateer, and that Captain Thomas was as bad a pirate as any. Bonnet ran up the *Jolly Roger* then, and went after any and all ships he saw. He had learned his lessons well from Blackbeard, and became known as a hard and cruel man, even though he still looked like a gentleman.

The *Royal James* was off the coast of North Carolina when the mate reported that repairs were needed. "I have men on the pumps all the time, Captain, but she's leaking worse and worse."

Stede stole a small ship to break up for planks to use in repairing the *Royal James*. Then he headed up the Cape Fear River. His men made camp on the shore, and put the ship into dry dock.

Down in Charles Town, people were still talking about the capture of Blackbeard. Lieutenant Maynard was the hero of the day, and they were sure that pirates would stay away from Charles Town from then on. They were angry when they learned that Captain Thomas and his *Royal James* were not far away.

Colonel William Rhett, who had done some pirate hunting in the past, went to Governor Johnson.

"Give me papers to capture pirates, Sir, and I'll bring in this Captain Thomas and any other pirates I find," Rhett told the governor.

Governor Johnson was more than willing to give the papers. Colonel Rhett was a rich man and would fit out his own ships. Soon two large sloops were ready, the *Henry* and the *Sea Nymph*. Colonel Rhett had eight guns fitted onto each of them, hired his crews and set sail, heading toward the Cape Fear River.

"We'll trap him there," he said. But he had to

depend upon his ships' mates to see that they found the river, for, like Stede Bonnet, Rhett was an army man, not a sailor.

The *Henry* and the *Sea Nymph* nosed into the river. They dropped anchor and sent a small boat ahead to spy out the place where the pirates were camped.

"It is not very far upriver," the scouts reported.

"Good," said Colonel Rhett. "We'll move in close, and drop anchor just one bend in the river below the pirate ship."

The mate of the *Henry* said, "Sir, I think we would do well to anchor right here."

"Oh, come now. There's no reason we can't go farther upstream. The water is deep enough," said Colonel Rhett.

"Yes, sir, it is now. But the tide is in. These Atlantic coast rivers rise and fall with the ocean tides, you know. When the tide goes out, we'll get trapped on a sandbar if we go farther upstream."

Colonel Rhett wanted to close in on the pirates in a narrower part of the river. He said, "We'll take a chance on it. I bought these sloops because I was told they would sail in shallow water. Now let's make use of them."

So on up the river they went, until they caught sight of the mast of the *Royal James* around the next bend. Anchors were dropped then. The mate had a worried look on his face.

"We've come too far upriver, sir. We should drop back. The tide is already falling."

"We'll be all right," said the colonel. "And the tide will rise again. We'll wait until then to make our attack."

Just then the mate saw the mate of the *Sea Nymph* signalling from the deck.

"Too late to drop back now," he said. "The *Sea Nymph* is already aground on a sand bar."

There came a soft sound from below the *Henry*.

"We're here to stay until the tide rises, whether we want to or not," said the mate.

The deck began to tilt a little as the water lowered. The *Henry* was plainly stuck. Even Landlubber Rhett could see that they had gone too far upstream. They settled down to wait until the tide would rise once more to set the ship free.

Up around the bend of the river, Landlubber Bonnet had the *Royal James* ready at last to move out to sea again. He had planned to get on the way the fol-

lowing morning when his scouts reported that two sloops were just below them in the river.

"Stuck fast on the sand bars, they are," reported the scouts, and laughed.

"Good," said Bonnet. "All we need to do is manage the *Royal James* well enough to slip past them before the tide sets them free. Get everything ready. We'll shoot holes in those two sloops as we pass and leave them there for good."

"I think we would do better to wait until the tide is rising, Captain," said Bonnet's mate.

"Then the enemy may be free, too, and will block us and shoot our hull full of holes before we get squared away to fire back. We'll go now. Get all set. I am counting on you to follow the deepest water of the river and get us past the two enemy ships."

So the mate had no choice. He followed Bonnet's orders, and soon the *Royal James* began its trip downstream. Just as the men stood ready to fire at the *Henry*, needing but a short distance more to be able to blast her tilted hull wide open, there came the sound of the keel slipping through mud. Sloo-oosh, and the *Royal James* was held as tightly as were the other two sloops.

"Bang! Bang!" came the fire of pistol shots.

"Take concealed positions and return the fire," ordered Bonnet.

The peppering of shot between the *Royal James* and the *Henry* went on and on, as men on each boat tried to catch someone on the enemy sloop in an open place. The decks tilted more and more. The *Henry* had the worst of it, for her decks were tilted toward the *Royal James,* making it harder for her men to hide.

For five hours, the peppering went on. Then the *Henry's* mate crawled over to where Rhett knelt, where the Landlubber Colonel had been trying for hours to get an open shot at the Landlubber Pirate. "Tide's coming in, Colonel Rhett," he reported. "Now we'll see who is first afloat."

Soon they could feel the *Henry* righting itself. Pistol firing from both ships stopped as the crews worked to get the sloops afloat. The current helped the *Henry* and the *Sea Nymph,* since they had gone into mud and sand as they went upstream. The men on the *Royal James* were still pushing desperately with poles, trying to get their sloop to back off the sand bar, working against the current, when the *Henry* and the *Sea Nymph* were both free.

"They're getting into position to give us a broadside

with their big guns, Captain," Bonnet's mate said. "We don't stand a chance. We may as well surrender before there is any killing."

Bonnet's mouth was set. I'll blow up the powder magazine before I'll surrender," he said.

The *Henry* was ready to send a volley of cannonballs. On her deck, Colonel Rhett stood with a speaking trumpet.

"Will you surrender, or do you choose to be blown to a watery grave?" he called out.

"Are you ready to fight, men?" Bonnet called out. He turned to look at his crew. Heads were shaking, and not one man was reaching for a gun.

"Be reasonable, Captain," the mate said. "We don't stand a chance. If we surrender, we can ask for pardons. Soon we will be back on the high seas. At worst, we will just be thrown into jail for awhile. These Carolina folks don't want to lose a chance to make money on stolen goods, and they won't cut off their noses to spite their faces."

Stede Bonnet saw that not one of his men wanted to fight. Maybe the mate was right, and they'd get off easily. He signaled surrender, and the *Jolly Roger* came down.

Off to Charles Town went the whole pirate crew. To their surprise, Governor Johnson proved to be not at all interested in making money from selling stolen pirate goods. The court he called together sentenced every man to die for the crimes of piracy.

The trial was short, and the hanging came right away, for all but Stede Bonnet.

Stede had days and days to wait in prison. He was well treated, for anyone could see that he had once lived the life of a gentleman. He saw a chance for escape once, and was gliding down the river in a canoe when Colonel Rhett came after him again. Four days later, he was tried, found guilty, and sentenced to be hanged.

The judge cleared his throat and began. "This man is found guilty of the worst crimes of piracy. He is hereby sentenced to be hanged by the neck until dead, within twenty-four hours."

Then he turned toward Bonnet. "Now, young man, I want you to think well of where you went wrong in the past, and how you can mend your life in the future. Surely you can live the kind of life that will earn you a greater reward than hanging. Think of a higher way of living than that of a blackguard pirate, sir, and plan your life to make up for your past . . . ."

The judge went on for a full hour, telling Bonnet how to lead a better life. As he talked, the sand in the hourglass sifted downward, marking the passing of Stede's last hours on earth. The prisoner squirmed and shifted from one foot to the other, wishing to have an end to the talk, talk, talk . . . .

Perhaps in those long minutes he wished he were back listening to the nagging of his wife in his pleasant West Indies home. Most surely, he must have wished he had blown himself out of earshot with one quick burst of the gunpowder on board the *Royal James*.

SILAS TALBOT, HEROIC PRIVATEER

The worst days of the pirates were over. Now and then a pirate ship was seen, but never again did pirates rule the seas as they had in the days of the buccaneers.

But each time there was a war, privateers sailed out to attack enemy ships, for there wasn't a big enough navy to do the work.

In America, privateers had a big job to do during the War for Independence, when the colonies were fighting for freedom from England. The brand new nation, the United States of America, had no navy or coast guard in its first days. As soon as possible, the government started a United States Navy, with warships and men to fight the battles at sea. But this took time. Without privateers, the War for Independence might never have been won.

Many men, working on privateers, fought bravely to help their new country. One such hero was a Massachusetts boy named Silas Talbot.

"I'm going to be a sailor," Silas said when he was still a small boy. His home was near the sea, and he

loved to watch the old, great square-riggers, the schooners, the smaller, swifter sloops and even the little fishing boats come in to the docks. He learned to tie a bowlin' and to coil a line. He made friends with the sailors who called to each other in loud voices that carried across the water of the bay.

When he was twelve, Silas talked a captain into taking him on as a cabin boy. The ship just worked the trade along the coast, but Silas learned all he could. Before many years he had become a ship's officer.

Silas left the sea when the call came in 1776 for men to fight for the rights of the American colonies. He was made captain of a regiment, and ordered to the Hudson River. He was in the army, but his first duty was on board a ship.

"Not that anyone will stay on this ship for long," Silas said, for he learned that the ship was what was called a "fire ship." An old ship was sometimes loaded with material that would burn easily. It was set on fire on purpose and pushed against an enemy warship with the idea that the burning ship might cause the warship to catch on fire, too, and perhaps explode.

The English ships were trying to work their way up the Hudson River at the same time that the soldiers on land were trying to capture the land along the river. The plan was that this would divide the New England people from those farther south. At the same time, other British ships were trying to stop all trading ships from going into and out of the harbors of American cities. Silas Talbot's fire ship was part of the plan to stop the English warships from going up the Hudson River.

"Captain Talbot, you are to be in charge of one of the three fire ships we are getting ready," he was told. "Your target ship will be the *Asia,* a large warship which carries 64 guns. It must be stopped before it gets very far up the river, or the plan to cut off New England might well succeed."

Silas and the men under him went to work on the fire ship. They took everything of any value off the old ship. Then they placed dry wood shavings, weeds and anything that would burn quickly along the deck. The dry old wood of the ship itself would make the best bonfire, but it had to be started burning all over, and fast. So they laid a "train" of rope soaked in turpentine from one end to the other of the decks. Along the way were charges of gunpowder to make explosions that would help spread the fire to the enemy ship.

The *Asia* moved up about seven miles above New

York City, which was in British hands. The time had come to stop the move up the river. Talbot and his little crew went on board their fire ship after dark, for its last ride down the river.

"It might be our last ride, too, if we don't get clear of it fast," Talbot said. "Once the fire reaches the gunpowder, we must be pulling upriver as hard as we can."

They had a small boat ready on the side of the fire ship which would be upriver from the *Asia*. They would jump into it as soon as they had lighted the "train." At the last minute, they sprinkled more gunpowder along the decks, and then poured turpentine on the whole thing. One boy offered to lie down on the deck, near the bow, right alongside the train to light it the moment the fire ship touched the *Asia*. If they lighted it too soon, the *Asia* would get clear of the fire ship's path and all their work would be wasted.

At two o'clock in the morning, the fire ship, with Talbot and his helpers on board, floated down the river. Silas himself would light one end of the train and his boy the other. The rest would get the small boat free of the fire ship and help the two fire-lighters get aboard. If the fire-lighters were slow in their work, all might die in the explosion.

Silently, they drifted down the river. Each man was praying, first that the *Asia* would not escape as they drew near, and then that they would escape the burning ship.

At last the men saw the dark shape of their target ship not far ahead.

"Ready, men?" Talbot whispered. "Another minute or two and we'll touch." Then he and Priestly, the boy who was going to light the bow end, crawled to their places, ready to start the fire. But as they did so, a flash of a firing gun and the sound of its shot broke the darkness and silence.

"They've seen us!" Silas muttered. He reached his place. Men on the *Asia* were firing at the ship as he and Priestly quickly did their work. The gunfire set off the explosions even before the train's sparks reached the piles of gunpowder. Before either Talbot or Priestly could roll off the deck into the blackness of the river water on the side away from the *Asia,* the fire ship was a wall of flame.

Talbot knew his clothes were flaming as he hit the water. Another second and he would have been trapped. He felt the pain of burns on his face and his hands and his body as he swam for his life. At the other end of the ship, Priestly was also heading for the rowboat. Willing hands pulled both men over the sides and into the boat, as flaming pieces of wood fell around them and into the rowboat itself.

Somehow they made it across the well-lighted waters to the shadows on the Jersey shore. They felt the boat touch bottom, and in a moment all of them were scrambling up the riverbank. Talbot felt pain in his eyes growing worse each second. And when, with the others, he turned to see what had become of the *Asia,* he could see nothing.

"Too bad they saw us," one of the men said, and he knew the *Asia* had not blown up. "I heard them pulling up the anchor even before that gunshot. They put a few feet between them and the fireship before the explosions could reach their gunpowder stores."

"They're still not in the clear, though," another said. "See? They're putting wet covers over their ammunition, and still beating out flames."

"But they've pushed what's left of the first ship clear of them with their grappling hooks. Too bad," said a voice Talbot knew was Priestly's. So the boy had been luckier than he, and could still see.

Later, they learned that they had hurt the *Asia*

enough to make her go back to New York harbor.

It was as they turned to make their way through the woods to a place where they could find shelter that they learned that Silas was badly burned and could not see. Carefully, they led him through the woods, and, as daylight came, up to a cottage. But there was no shelter there, for the lady who opened the door was so frightened at the sight of the blackened men that she screamed and slammed the door in their faces. The same thing happened at several other houses. Finally, a woman living alone in a one room log cabin saw that these were Americans in need of help. She let them in. Silas stayed there for several weeks, until his eyes and the worst of his burns were healed and he could join his army regiment once more.

But the army was not for Silas Talbot. He was too quick to rush into action, and again and again he was wounded. He was sent to his home in Providence, Rhode Island, to get well, and his time in the army was over.

He was getting well again when he heard that the British were going to try to take his home city, attacking it from the river.

"Not if I can help it," Silas announced. "I'll get a

letter of marque as a privateer and see to it myself."

He fitted out a little schooner with two cannons that shot three-pound cannon balls and found sixty men willing to fight with him.

To get to Providence by water, a ship went through a bay with many islands in it, and then up the Providence River. The largest island is the one from which the state of Rhode Island takes its name. The Providence River branches off northwest of Rhode Island. Another river is on the east side of the island. Into this bay and the river on the east side came a British ship named the *Pigot.*

On the *Pigot's* decks were eight big cannons, shooting twelve-pound cannon balls, and ten smaller cannons. Instead of being the old kind that pointed only out to the side of the ship, they were of a kind which could be pointed in almost any direction.

Talbot, fitting out his ship at Providence, sent scouts down to see what the British were doing and what kind of ship was coming to take the city.

The scouts reported, "We never can climb onto her decks, Captain. There is a tangle of nets all around to stop anyone who tries it."

"H-mmmmmm," said Silas. "How many men on board?"

"Not many that I could see. Maybe forty, maybe fifty."

Silas looked at his little schooner, the *Hawk,* with its two tiny cannons.

"One thing is clear already," he said. "We shall have to use our heads, since we can't take it by strength. But, one way or another, we'll stop the *Pigot* before she gets to Providence."

He began to plan what he would do. First he had to get by the British soldiers who were in trenches watching the river at the north end of Rhode Island. That was the first step. When the wind was right, he set sail. Down the Providence River went the little *Hawk.* It came to the end of the river, and into the bay. The guns of the British soldiers were pointed down at it. The bay was wide, fortunately, and the fire of the guns did not quite reach across it.

"Bang! Bang!" The firing stirred up the water beside the *Hawk.*

"Keep her moving, and close to the shore!" Captain Talbot ordered. The schooner raced along, full speed. Once it seemed she would be stopped, but only a few boards on the ship's side were splintered. She turned up the river that emptied into the bay at the northeast corner. Silas knew this river, the Taunton, very well, for his boyhood home was only a few miles upstream.

"Won't they know what we are up to, now that they have seen us?" asked one of the men.

Silas laughed. "Who would think a little mosquito like the *Hawk* would attack a big wasp such as the *Pigot?* No, they will not worry about the likes of us."

They went six miles up the Taunton, there to wait for the right time to travel fifteen miles southward to where the *Pigot* lay anchored on the east side of Rhode Island.

In the morning, Silas said, "I am going down to have a look at that ship myself."

He borrowed a horse and rode down to the shore opposite the *Pigot.* From the edge of a bluff, he studied the ship carefully through a spyglass. Minutes went by as he stood there. Then he lowered the glass and spoke aloud, "By jinks, I believe we can do it. We'll get rid of those nettings, and then we can board her."

Back he went to the *Hawk,* and then to a near-by army camp where he asked for fifteen more men. When all the men were gathered on the *Hawk,* Silas explained his plan.

As he finished he said, "Now, men, the most important thing is for us to keep cool. And there will be a reward for the first man who sets foot on the deck of the *Pigot.*"

"Hurray!" shouted the men. The plan was so daring that each man felt keyed up and excited. Looking at them, Silas knew that if his plan failed, it would not be the fault of these brave men.

At nine o'clock that night they raised the *Hawk's* anchor and let the river current carry them downriver, aided by sails and oars. But as they came near a British fort which was just about four miles upriver from the *Pigot,* they dropped the sails. Their whiteness might make the schooner noticed from the fort on the bluff.

"There are the guards," a lieutenant whispered to Talbot. "Do you think they'll see us?"

Silas watched the men marching slowly along the top of the thick wall of the fort. He could see them plainly when they passed some lighted windows of a big building behind the wall.

The *Hawk* slipped silently along through the water. Not a man spoke until they were well below the fort.

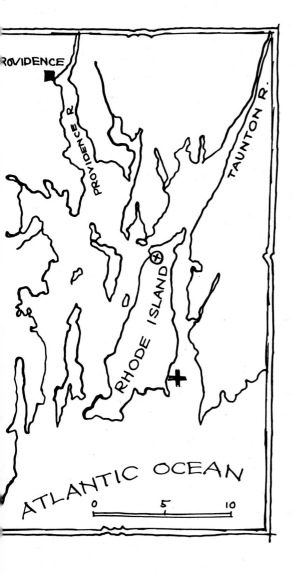

PROVIDENCE

PROVIDENCE R.

TAUNTON R.

RHODE ISLAND ⊕

ATLANTIC OCEAN

0   5   10

⊗ FIRST PORT TO
   BE PASSED

■ SECOND PORT
   TO BE PASSED

✛ LOCATION OF
   THE PIGOT

Then, when they could breathe easily once more, they raised their canvas and moved more swiftly on toward the *Pigot*. The night had become very black, and Silas could not make out any landmarks at all.

"We should be close by now, men," he said. "Keep silence from here on. We'll drop anchor and I'll go in the small boat to look for the ship."

He climbed down into the little rowboat that was pulled along behind the *Hawk,* taking along cloth to wrap around the oarlocks so that there would be no telltale squeaks. He had rowed only a short distance when suddenly a big black shape was before him. He had found the *Pigot*. He sat quietly for several minutes, listening, trying to decide if the ship had changed its position since he had studied it from the bluff. Then he went back to the *Hawk*.

"Ready, men," he said. He took the wheel himself, and steered the *Hawk* toward the *Pigot*. On the *Hawk's* bow was attached a strong pole. To the outer end of this pole, Silas had fastened the kind of anchor that has sharp hooks on it. With this, they were going to hook the netting on the *Pigot* and rip it out of the way, making an open place where the men could board the big ship. Each man sat ready now, with his rifle, his pistols and his knife at hand for the fight that was sure to come.

"Who goes there?" came the call as the *Hawk* moved into the shadow of the *Pigot.*

Deep silence. The attackers hardly dared breathe. But on the *Pigot,* somebody heard the rippling of the water. A peppering of musket fire splattered into the water.

"Lie low," whispered Talbot, and the men were not hurt.

The anchor hook did its work well. It ripped away a great length of the netting. Some men were to hook the two ships together, and this they did without trouble.

The lieutenant who had brought the company of fifteen men from the army camp was first on board the *Pigot.* In a moment, each man was in hand-to-hand combat with the men who were on duty on the *Pigot's* deck.

Shouts of alarm rang out, and the ship's commander, Lieutenant Dunlop, came climbing onto the deck, in his underwear.

"What goes on here?" he cried.

Silas pulled his sword. "Surrender, sir. Your ship is in the hands of the United States Government." The

officer found himself in the center of a ring of grim-faced but happy Americans, each pointing a gun at him. The rest of the attackers had the *Pigot's* crew under control.

Talbot pulled his letters of marque from his pocket and opened them before Lieutenant Dunlop.

"In the daylight, you will see that I am a licensed privateersman," he said. "The *Pigot* is my prize. We will deliver you into the hands of a general of the United States Army, under the rules of warfare. Now, sir, if you will follow your men below —"

As had been planned, the *Hawk's* men were forcing all of the *Pigot's* men to go below, down the ship's ladder. Lieutenant Dunlop had no choice but to follow them. He still did not know the size of the "mosquito" privateer that had taken his big ship, without killing a man on either side.

Just as he started down the ladder, he asked Talbot, "What ship has taken us?"

Talbot grinned. "The *Hawk,* sir, seventy tons, carrying two three pounders, and manned mostly by soldiers."

Dunlop groaned. "There goes my hope for a promotion."

He went below. Talbot's men bound the hatch

closed with ropes. The soldiers, many of whom had gone to sea in the days before the war, took over the stations on the ship. As daylight came, the little *Hawk* moved proudly downstream, seeming to be towing the great *Pigot* behind her. Talbot did not dare try to pass the fort again, for fear of losing all he had won, so the prisoners were taken to the nearest safe landing place and turned over to the army, to be marched back to Providence.

Silas Talbot spent the rest of the war years working as a privateersman. He joined the many others who went out on the open sea, doing his part in helping to let American ships and those of her friends get into and out of the harbors. Without the work of the privateers, the new little nation might never have won her freedom.

Privateering was still needed as a help to the United States Navy when the War of 1812 was fought. But steadily, the young government built up its strength at sea so that never again could sea robbers such as the buccaneers set foot on United States land. While George Washington was still president, the United States Coast Guard had its start. Congress voted in 1790, to fit out a fleet of ten sloops to keep back any pirates who might still try to slip into the sheltering coves of the American coast line.

The last American privateersman did his work during the War Between the States. Privateers disappeared along with the old wooden battleships, after the battle between the *Monitor* and the *Merrimac* proved that ships with steel sides made much better fighting ships to protect the nation. Another frontier had passed.

Now the United States Navy, Marine Corps and Coast Guard, with the help of the Merchant Marine, are well able to protect our shores and fight our sea battles. Even fierce old Blackbeard would not stand a chance today. The book is closed on pirates and privateers.